TIMELESS WISDOMS

volume two

Reflections of Spirit

L.L.
Dr. John-Roger

TIMELESS WISDOMS

volume two

Reflections of Spirit

John-Roger, D.S.S.
with photographs by David Sand

Mandeville Press
Los Angeles, California

Mandeville Press
P.O. Box 513935
Los Angeles, California 90051-1935
323-737-4055
jrbooks@mandevillepress.org
www.mandevillepress.org

Printed in the United States of America
ISBN: 978-1-893020-51-1
LCCN: 2008910401

Other Books by John-Roger, D.S.S.

Blessings of Light
The Consciousness of Soul
Divine Essence
Dream Voyages
Forgiveness – The Key to the Kingdom
Fulfilling Your Spiritual Promise
God Is Your Partner
Inner Worlds of Meditation
Journey of a Soul
Living Love from the Spiritual Heart
Loving Each Day
Loving Each Day for Moms & Dads
Loving Each Day for Peacemakers
Manual on Using the Light
Momentum: Letting Love Lead (with Paul Kaye)
Passage Into Spirit
The Path to Mastership
The Power Within You
Psychic Protection
Relationships: Love, Marriage and Spirit
The Rest of Your Life (with Paul Kaye)
Sex, Spirit and You
The Spiritual Family
Spiritual High (with Michael McBay, M.D.)
The Spiritual Promise
Spiritual Warrior: The Art of Spiritual Living
The Tao of Spirit
Timeless Wisdoms
Walking with the Lord
The Way Out Book
Wealth & Higher Consciousness
What's It Like Being You? (with Paul Kaye)
When Are You Coming Home? (with Pauli Sanderson)

Foreword

Most people would probably agree that we live in trying times, and even when the environment is relatively calm, each of us has personally trying times. Life just seems to be like this for humans. Dr. John-Roger has said that we can go through life laughing or crying, and in *Timeless Wisdoms, Reflections of Spirit,* he offers a path through, a way to look at life and ourselves from a higher altitude—a way to laugh even in the midst of the challenges.

Just how to choose or even see the possibility of laughter, joy, and love is something John-Roger has written about in over fifty books, and this approach starts with his basic idea: "With loving, you can overcome all things." And he teaches that the source of that loving is within us. We can call it the Soul, the God within, the Beloved, the spiritual heart. The term doesn't matter, but the experience of it does, and John-Roger has been teaching people how to do this for 45 years.

The inspiring selections in *Timeless Wisdoms, Reflections of Spirit,* come to the essence of many of the things John-Roger has shared, and they can help us remember the truth about ourselves whenever we forget. Perhaps you might meditate on one thought and see what that awakens in you. You could use one of the selections as a guiding focus for the day and become aware of how you view yourself, others, and the world from that perspective. You could contemplate one of the beautiful photographs and experience where that takes you inside yourself.

Above all, as John-Roger says here, "Let your love be your guiding star. Let it be in your breath. Then you live in the heart of God, all things are made new, and God is personally present, all the time."

Betsy Alexander

Living love means that your love extends unconditionally to all things.
You love everything present, no exceptions.

The face of God is in everything you experience. The face of God is never hidden from you. You only hide it from yourself when you do not look at what is so, when you do not look at reality, when you pretend that you can make some ideal of yours supersede what reality is.

The energy of living love can give courage and hope. It can renew the faith of everyone around. Find your center of living love, and give from that level.

Pure love is the Soul.

Ask for the Light, and then keep your eyes open to see what the Light shines on for your immediate level of concern.

As you exercise freedom, you learn to be responsible for what you create and thus are educated by your own experience.

When you come to those peak experiences wherein you find love residing,
identify them, internalize them, and make them glow so that you can find them again
when you start to go off your path. Go into those loving places often,
and build that strong place within where you can say,
"God and I are one."

Man's prime direction is to understand his own beingness. That's a full-time job.

There's only one key, only one law, and that is the law of loving.

What's the hardest—and most important—thing
we have to do as people who are following Christ,
people who are following God, people who are
following love? We've got to be forgiving.

It is the Soul that endures past all things.

Disturbing action creates karma. Disturbing reaction perpetuates karma. If you change disturbing action to love and disturbing reaction to acceptance and understanding, you can experience love, joy, peace, and fulfillment. These divine attributes do not disturb the harmony of God's creation.

Remember that God's time, not
your time, is always perfect.

Do the next thing in front of you to do, and do it lovingly.
Pray to be guided by God and to be aware of that guidance,
and then live your life as lovingly as you can.

Home is where the Spirit of Christ reigns eternally, and that is in the heart.
Where there is love, there we have found home.

"As you sow, so also shall you reap" can be a highly spiritual action—where a positive action leads to a positive result. So hold on to the image of what you want. On the physical, imaginative, and spiritual levels, create and express that which is positive and uplifting, and then you can reap what you have sowed.

When you reach into the unconditional energy of Spirit, you don't experience love; you are love.

The Light of the Soul emanates from the center of your being as living love. The Soul is noninflictive by nature. The Soul is joyful. The Soul is a divine river from the infinite Ocean of Love and Mercy.

You cannot be shut off from God. You can only think you are.

Don't be afraid to look at yourself.
If something's wrong, find out now. Even if you've spent
thirty years expressing a particular way, if it's wrong,
it's wrong. Drop it. If you're smart, you'll let it go so fast
that everybody will wonder what happened.

Once you enter the Divine presence, you no longer worry about the past or the future. You are able to say, "Tomorrow? What is tomorrow? What's next week? What's next year? Does it matter if I am here or there? Wherever I am, I will be in this loving, radiant peace that illuminates all things."

Those who sit quietly in the silence that roars the name of the Lord and do the most mundane jobs in love and devotion are performing a beautiful service that God sees as very great, indeed.

There is something transcendental in the process of giving love. It is your very beingness that speaks when you are loving.

It is a challenge to take that which has been your hurt, your anger, your grief, and use these as stepping-stones to go higher in your spiritual freedom.

Dig deeply into the spring of love and partake of it.
The supply is infinite.

If you have established peace within your own consciousness, no one can take that from you.

Often, in stepping back from the tree that we beat our heads against, we can see the pathway through the forest. Then our approach becomes active or self-directed, not reactive. In Soul consciousness, we get above the forest and see where the trail is and what's in there; we walk very happily through the forest, being of service, knowing we can get out, knowing there's nothing in there that we can't handle. Karma, on the other hand, is going through it in fear of the darkness, creating monsters that don't exist.

I know that it can be a challenge at times to hold the positive focus and to continue to put out love, no matter what. This doesn't mean you have to be a fool and let people walk all over you and take advantage of you—not at all. It does mean that you do not return anger with anger, hurt with another hurt, or a name with another name.

Live in the truth of your own beingness, and let your actions speak for you.

Our "natural" state is loving. We don't have to wait for any divine miracle to occur.

Within you is the kingdom of God. You have the key. As you awaken more fully to the consciousness of God, you find that there is no love or lover. There is only the Beloved.

Forgiveness is one of the main doorways into grace and loving.

The only thing we can do on the planet is the best we can. People do things the best they can, and then they say it wasn't the best they could. And if they are given another chance, they will do it the same way the second time—and a third, a fourth, a fifth, and a sixth time. What you might say to them is, "If you could have done better, you would have done better, and you did the best you could."

Remember that we are of God. We walk through this life with God beside us as our guide. We are never alone, never separated, always loved and cared for. We are one in God's heart.

If you have a spiritual experience and you want to keep having spiritual experiences, you must turn from that which you just completed and go on to the next thing. To do less is to deny your growth and awareness.

As you focus on the outer world, you may see imbalance and disease. But there is no need to reside in that because there is a place inside you wherein resides serenity.

Every day we create new through change by flowing with what is present.

If, indeed, you can be taught, the Soul will awaken itself on the physical level and dissolve all karmic bondage. Then you will be aware of Soul on this level and on all other levels. At that moment, you become what we call one of the "living free."

Right now is all that really exists for us. If you begin with what's true for you in this moment and work with that and don't focus on negative things in the past that have "gone wrong," you may find that things will begin clearing.

You can keep the awareness of
the Light and of God present in
your heart, no matter what. When
you do, you stand as a beacon of
Light for everyone around you.

In Spirit, there is no time and no space. All exists right now, in eternity. All exists as one. There is no division, no separation. One Soul is all Souls. These realizations do not come with mentalizing or verbalization; they come from the intelligence of the Soul, from the knowledge inherent within you.

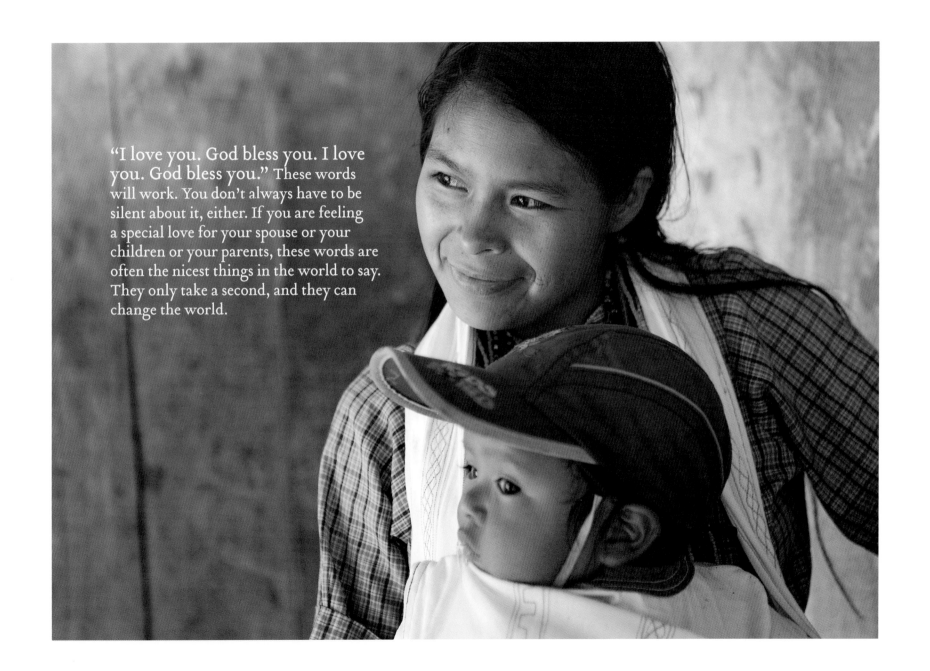

"I love you. God bless you. I love you. God bless you." These words will work. You don't always have to be silent about it, either. If you are feeling a special love for your spouse or your children or your parents, these words are often the nicest things in the world to say. They only take a second, and they can change the world.

Spirit is joyful. The nature of the Soul is joyful.
The personality isn't always joyful, but it is part of
the illusions of the physical level.

When we start to become
whole and complete,
the goodness of God in us
starts to flow up and out; it
takes the personality and lifts
it up. That doesn't mean that
the negative side won't still
nag away at us. But if we
acknowledge the negative
side, it will lose its power
and will cease to control us.

The chief intention of spiritual warriors is to become aware of their spiritual nature. I have stated my own intention this way: "I'm keeping my eyes on You, Lord, only You." You may want to put this intention into different words, but the basic idea will be the same for us all.

Be devoted to yourself.

We have the power to create peaceful relationships with ourselves, our spouses, our children, our relatives, and the entire human family, regardless of race, creed, color, gender, or nationality. Easy? No, but it can be simple. It takes great courage, which is the energy of the heart.

When you ask for inner peace, you may find yourself talking less. To find the peace within, it's often necessary to be quiet so that you can hear the inner voice of love.

Realize that each person's way is special for that person. Don't compare levels of what you call spirituality. Sit and listen and support each person with your love and your joy for them. Then move back to your own truth, to your own work, to your own beingness.

When you become one with life, the very leaves on the trees are the scripture of nature. The face you look at is the scripture of your own beingness. The aura around you is the scripture of your mind and emotions and, very often, of your own spirituality. The very Soul is seeing the face of God in the physical world.

Experience your own divinity.

See if there are some areas where you can lighten up. One of the best ways to relieve tension is with humor. It's never too late to have a happy childhood.

Don't look for God and Spirit outside yourself; just awaken to the presence inside. Know that God reigns personally inside you as you, and the Beloved is present. We are one in God's loving heart, and there is truly only one Beloved: the God-form. You are part of it. Everyone is.

There is a guide inside you, a great counselor, a guiding Light. God is present, working in you as you, pulling your consciousness away from the distractions of the world and back into awareness of Spirit.

The Wind that blows from heaven is the Sound of God, and that is what we call the Christ.

If you hear inner answers, it's okay if you check them out, but don't just trust them without checking. If they give direction, lean into that direction, see how it feels and how it works for you. If something works for you, it doesn't matter where you get the information. And if it doesn't work for you, it also doesn't matter where you got the information. The criterion is whether or not it works, not where the information came from.

If you stay focused in the now, you can have tremendous joy and great fun wherever you find yourself. It's all your attitude, and your attitude is your choice.

The important thing is not so much whether
you are in a male body or a female body now,
not so much your circumstances, but what
you make of them: how much you learn,
how much you grow, and, especially,
how much you love.

Blaze a path inside you that leads to love and joy. Foster and nurture all the positive aspects of yourself. Dwell on that which is good.

It's in the reaching out, the loving, the caring, the touching, and the sharing of our hearts that we truly receive.

Sometimes doing nothing is the greatest gift you can give to another.
Sometimes just your presence is the greatest gift.

You are always in your own movement of spiritual inner awareness.
You can come together with other people to assist each other
as part of this movement.

Recognize the divine Soul within every person you meet.

When you recognize that the Soul is perfect and complete, you have found your "Soul mate." When you recognize that you are complete, then you have no need for the boundaries of this world. And this is what is often called self-realization. It's freedom.

Love can appear in all sorts of forms.
It can appear as discipline. It can appear
as limitation. It can appear as freedom. It
doesn't have just one expression.

Laugh and smile in the midst of contraction, but be more bold—not in terms of risking, but be more bold in terms of trusting yourself, trusting more to the Lord, following the inner guidance, not your emotional feelings about things.

Love is the key to awakening to the Spirit within.

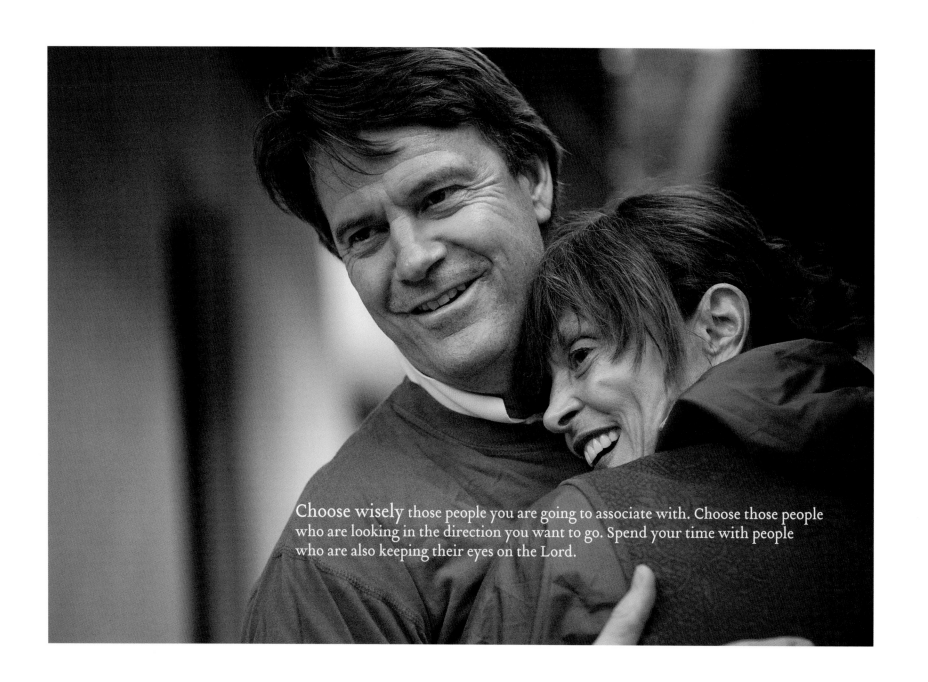

Choose wisely those people you are going to associate with. Choose those people who are looking in the direction you want to go. Spend your time with people who are also keeping their eyes on the Lord.

You can know happiness, and you can know love.
There is nothing else as worthwhile knowing.
Love is the only channel for clear communication,
and love is the parent of peace.

If you can stop for a moment in your thinking and your questing and listen to the silence, you may start becoming aware of many levels of consciousness. You may become aware that you are on all levels of Light simultaneously. The "trick" is to learn to shift your awareness to where you wish to be.

When we get high enough in the consciousness of God, we all have the same name. And that name is Love.

The heart wants a contentment, a peacefulness, a quality of flowing through life like a stream that flows on its path to the ocean. You're flowing on the stream of Light and Sound, into this great ocean of love. You can't get off. You can go a long way to the periphery, but you still keep moving forward. And everyone is going to make it back to the ocean, back into the heart of God.

Let us create words of harmony, pleasure, and love. Let us create thoughts that are worthy of the Divinity within each of us. Let us create love that can be manifested anywhere, at any time. Let us walk with the Beloved and just be one with all.

You're in the physical body, but you are not it. You are on the planet, but you are not the planet. It's a truth and a paradox that everything you are to become, you are right now.

You can be honest and true to yourself without making anyone else wrong.

The holy land is wherever divine love is being made manifest. And wherever you demonstrate the consciousness of love, that land becomes sacred and holy.

Give of the goodness that you are. Give of the truth that you are. Give of the Spirit that you are. The reward will be that you know those aspects of yourself more deeply and truly. The Spirit will become more alive and present for you in every moment, and you will walk hand in hand with the Beloved and know yourself and God as one.

The Christ within you
knows the Christ in others.
To many people, the Christ has
not appeared yet. To others, he
has come and gone. But those
who dwell in it know the
Christ is eternally present.

The Kingdom of Heaven is found in the place of your compassion. It's found in the place of your loving. It's found in the place of your generosity. It's found in the place of your healing of yourself and others. It's very easy to find the Kingdom of Heaven inside.

When you release your desire for something, your unhappiness goes. When you release the concern about what somebody else thinks about something, your concern about it goes. As you realize that you can't handle other people's lives, your worry about them goes. And when you realize that you can handle your own life, your happiness increases.

Don't be concerned that what is so for today doesn't feel like what was so yesterday. The Light will keep disturbing things enough to keep you reaching up so that you don't forget to grow. The Light will comfort the disturbed and disturb the comfortable. Just keep flowing with what is, because you're just going to keep lifting into new things.

When you are in acceptance, you are in profound peace. Accepting something doesn't mean you are agreeing with it or condoning it. In acceptance, you are freeing yourself of negative thoughts and feelings and making yourself available to the powerful presence of peace. You can see more clearly. This is the place you want to be in when you have decisions to make. This is the place from which you can make an impact on the world for the better.

When children need something, they come to you to fulfill their prayers. They are depending on you to see what you can do to fulfill them. Don't be afraid to pick them up, cuddle them, love them, rub their backs, and kiss and hug them. Give them all the love you can muster, and they will return it to you in more ways than you can imagine.

The family is the foundation of society. Love is the foundation
of the family. God is the foundation of love.

If you want to change anything or anyone, change it inside yourself.

The potential for peace is in the human genetic code, but it is not activated in many people. It is being activated in those who are moving into a higher consciousness, which includes peace.

If you want to be an optimist, if you want your energies to be lifting, if you want to realize your highest potential for joy and fulfillment, then you must pledge to yourself that from this moment, you will become more and more aware of what you are doing now.

Life is awareness. Life is love.

Let the Christ be born in you.

There is only one mind, and that is the mind of God. There is only one love, and that is the love of God. There is only one consciousness, and that is the consciousness of God.

You can evoke the spiritual form of the Christ within your consciousness. It's easy because you are a child of God, as we are all children of God. You are heir to divinity. It is your birthright.

You can know happiness,
and you can know love.
Seek these things inside, and
then you will start perceiving
them around you.

The more you are loving, the more you free yourself to experience the Soul.

As your expression becomes more closely matched with the inner integrity of your being, you find yourself moving into the Christ of your inner consciousness. It's a place that has no description, although it may be the greatest level of reality you have ever known. As you move to that reality, it is like paying your true self a visit. It's like coming home inside of yourself. The joy, bliss, and ecstasy that can come forward from that small visit with your true self can carry you through some very rough spots in your life.

You are divine love.
You are living love.

It is important to take time for yourself each day—
time to focus into your spiritual awareness, time to drop the physical concerns of the moment
and once again become aware that you are spiritual, that you are divine,
that you are, through your Soul, an extension of the Supreme God.

Has your attitude slipped? Correct it by positive doing.

As you create expectations of people
or situations, as you create opinions of
what should or should not be taking
place with yourself and others, you
create your dilemmas.

There is one God. There is one intelligence,
which is God's intelligence. There is one body,
which is God's body. You are a part of God. You are
an extension of spiritual energy.

We must see within ourselves and inquire
within ourselves to find understanding.

Listen to the heart, which will tell you truly where you live. When you turn to the heart, which the Light has filled to overflowing, you know the joy of the world.

If you look deeply into people, you will see something very majestic.

Love God with all your heart. Love yourself with the same devotion. Love all who come to you as you love God. But practice finding the loving within yourself first before you look out. With loving, nothing is impossible.

Love is living in the spiritual heart.

The spiritual Light illuminates the lower levels and guides you into experiences which allow you to learn, to grow, to lift into a more direct awareness of Spirit.

My Beloved, it is just a while longer that you are here.
Can you not endure all things to find the Kingdom of Heaven?

Put the Light around the world. Ask to live each moment in the consciousness of the Light and to be the Light.

When you just love, with no restrictions, no qualifications, no conditions, you'll be so happy and joyful that you'll have a hard time containing it all.

Spirit is not a process of the outer world,
although Its qualities may be reflected here in kindness, loving,
and compassion.

The best approach is simply to live in the now, do the best you can with your present abilities and talents, and let your actions speak for themselves. That takes understanding and awareness. It also takes love and respect for yourself. With it comes freedom, a sense of self-worth, and an inner security and serenity that is worth everything.

Reach within yourself to the source of knowledge and strength, and know for yourself what is right to do.

The person who understands you the most, who cares for you the most, who can do the most for you, is you. The ultimate relationship is with yourself, and it's important to keep that inner relationship harmonious. To do that, you have to be in a continual state of self-education, and you need to tune in to the source of who you really are.

Our work, if we accept it, is to bring our consciousness into the higher understanding, into experiencing and knowing the Christ within.

Every Soul
has the
divine message
within itself.

It is the Soul that endures past all things.

Gain the knowledge and the understanding of your true self,
and you will be able to live your life from a position of wisdom.

Just remain neutral. Come in, listen to the teachings, don't believe or disbelieve, just listen. See what works for you, start working it, see what happens. If it's not for you, you'll find out pretty fast.

You cannot be shut off from God—you can only think you are.

When you connect to the presence of Spirit inside you,
the teachings are given to you inwardly and become an
aspect of your experience.

If you don't learn something everyday, what are you doing, anyway?

Let love be your guide, your breath, your life. Then you live in the heart of God and are renewed every moment through His love.

I pray, Father,
that I hold peace and
love in my heart.
And I ask for strength
that through my
loving, through my
caring, and through
my sharing, I may
extend the Light of
love and peace to
all I meet.

If you want to find Spirit everywhere you go, take it with you.

Always use love all ways.

God is everywhere, in all things and in all levels of consciousness.
Things that appear to be negative are only learning devices, not punishments.

Charity reflects the loving that is the very essence behind all creation.
There is nowhere that it is not.

After you've completed the pathway you're on and you see no more Light
ahead of you, stop and go within. Recharge the battery.
Spiritual exercises and meditation will point you back to the stability
of the spiritual life.

Take a few moments just to appreciate your body for the way it has always served you. You are simply loving and appreciating your body, just the way it is.

Learn all you can from every experience and just go on.

Make peace with yourself. Forgive yourself for all the times
you haven't done your best, no matter what the reason.
Forgive yourself for forgetting that you are divine.

There will come a time in the Soul of everyone on this planet
when they will receive the divine Light and know it.

Each time you can look into an area of your unhappiness and see how it can be changed, you come closer to the realization of your divinity.

Ignorance is a "sin," the only sin. When you come into understanding, the ignorance drops away and you change automatically.

Complete the projects you begin,
fulfill the commitments you have made,
live up to the promises you have made.

When you don't have sufficient energy and you're too tired, look at what you've started and what you haven't completed. Every one of those projects demands a level of your energy.

You have to actively place yourself in a position to receive what you want.

As God in manifestation, we are responsible for what we create.

Have the wit to look at an area and say, "This causes me trouble."
It takes courage to walk away from the familiar thing that is not
working for you, into the unfamiliar thing wherein you may find
your eternal happiness.

If you marry because you love the other person and it doesn't matter what they do, then that is the marriage that can endure and be enjoyed throughout all experiences for a lifetime.

Loving is the most important quality you can nurture in yourself.

God may be using your family, friends, boss, or even total strangers to bring discipline to you, but it is really coming from Spirit. Spirit loves you enough to point up to you the mistakes you are making and to assist you in correcting them.

Christ-mass, or Christmas, is not the exchanging of a gift out there,
but a receiving of the gift of the Christ into you.

We can think we are perfectly justified in stopping
our loving for a variety of reasons—boredom, irritation,
anger, hurt, etc.—but loving is always the baseline of
life, the thing that is more important than anything else.

You cannot allow anything discourteous to get into your mental attitude towards anything or anyone, including yourself. The instant you do, your relationship goes out of balance. There is no emotionalism, no sentimentality, no wishful thinking in all of this. You simply realize that if you identify anything as either intelligent or unintelligent, good or bad, friendly or unfriendly, cooperative or uncooperative, that is precisely how it will appear, for all you experience is the state of your own consciousness being made manifest in your outward experience.

When people say things meant to hurt or anger you, you don't have to fight them. You don't have to do anything. Let them have their fun. You simply direct yourself into the consciousness that you want to have.

Soul Transcendence is a simple path. There is nothing extraordinary you need to do. Simply open your awareness to all that is around you and all that is within you, and follow the loving.

Let your love be your guiding star. Let it be in your breath. Then you live in the heart of God, all things are made new, and God is personally present, all the time.

The spiritual warrior does not just listen to anything and everything. They take the sword of truth and use that to "cut" the information. But the sword is the heart.

When you are expressing the love and the Light within you and then someone starts to hit against you, sit down, call in the Light, and ask for the power of the Spirit to be placed around you for protection and guidance. It will be there for you.

Tune in to divine love—the center where you know goodness dwells, the place where you are truly alive and from which you express calmly, peacefully, and with love. When this process starts, you are opening the portals of your Soul.

If you want to know Soul Transcendence, forgive people. This doesn't mean you become stupid and don't see the injustice or the negativity of the situation. It means that you walk towards a Light consciousness, a transcendent consciousness. You walk towards God. And as you do that, you may see more clearly what is actually happening.

Love is the greatest step of mastership. When loving is expressed, all other aspects of mastership fall into place and blend into the loving. It is the greatest of the keys.

We're vital, alive human beings, and part of our existence here is loving, caring, and sharing. Cultivate what works for you in every area—emotionally, financially, physically—all of it. Take good care of yourself. Then you can give from the overflow of your loving and abundance.

It is time to come back into your heart, into that one place that is the essence of who you are, into that one place that continually vibrates, "I am love."

Whenever you hear of any negativity, instead of adding to it by condemning the people involved, send Light and love to everyone—even to those who have "messed up." Start adding peace into the situation through your compassion, acceptance, and understanding.

When you experience God, you experience love, the love that transcends all the physical limitations and touches into your deepest, most sacred place, and you know you are in the presence of your divinity. Loving is of greatest value to you.

We work with the Light of God in a process of living love. If you follow any path and do not find the love of God on that path, then leave it and seek out one that carries the love. There must be love of God and love for God. There must be love for the Light consciousness that comes through all people, for that is God.

Don't expect other people to make you happy;
make your own happiness. Then you'll be
shining forth the spiritual love.

It's your attitude towards what you are doing that counts—
not just what you are doing, but your attitude towards it.

It is important to take responsibility for your actions. It becomes more and more difficult to lay your troubles at somebody else's doorstep and say, "My misery is your fault." No, your misery is only your choice. Your joy is also your choice.

When you give of your ability, your joy, your gifts, and your creativity, people coming behind you (whom you may not even know) are able to partake of the blessings you extend.

You bring to yourself that which you focus upon,
so it makes sense to focus on the best, the highest thing you know.

Come into the process of understanding, and maintain your calm by consciously, directly holding and not letting flights of fancy take you where they will. Come back to this moment continually, and you'll find that tensions and distractions disappear, and you'll start coming into the calmness of right now.

If you seek the Kingdom of Heaven, you're going to find it.
If you don't seek it, you are still going to find it; it's just going to take a little longer.

It matters little what someone else does or has done.
What matters is what you're doing right now.

The movement of spiritual inner awareness teaches the awakening in love.

As you begin your inner journey, you will be filled with joy and the glorious feeling of love.

Whenever you let go, you will probably find that you have made a space for something greater to happen. When you let go of resentment, you'll have more energy for appreciation. And when you let go of your attachment to outcomes, you will have more energy to enjoy and participate in this very moment.

About the Author

For more than forty years, Dr. John-Roger's life has been devoted to the spiritual work of Soul Transcendence, the realization of oneself as a Soul and, as one with the Divine. In the course of his work, he has traveled and spoken extensively throughout the world and written over fifty books, two of which have been on the *New York Times* Best-seller List. He has given over six thousand talks, and many are presented on his nationally seen television show, "That Which Is."

John-Roger, D.S.S. is the founder and spiritual advisor of the nondenominational Church of the Movement of Spiritual Inner Awareness (MSIA); founder, first president, and now chancellor of the University of Santa Monica; founder and president of Peace Theological Seminary & College of Philosophy; founder and chairman of the board of Insight Seminars; founder and first president of the Institute for Individual and World Peace; and founder of the Heartfelt Foundation.

John-Roger's wisdom, humor, common sense, and love have helped people discover the Spirit within themselves and find greater health, prosperity, and peace, and he continues to transform lives by educating people in the wisdom of the spiritual heart.

For more information about John-Roger, you may also visit: www.john-roger.org

Fulfilling Your Spiritual Promise

If you ever had a question for John-Roger, chances are you'll find it answered here.

This 3-volume set of books by Dr. John-Roger is a compendium of information he has shared over many years. Along with an index that makes finding topics easy, its 24 chapters include a wealth of information on subjects including karma, the Mystical Traveler, initiation, and dreams, as well as attitude, relationships, health, and practical spirituality. And at just $45 for the whole set, this resource is a great buy. (ISBN: 978-1-893020-17-7. Hardbound, 3-book set, $45)

To order this book or other materials by John-Roger, contact the Movement of Spiritual Inner Awareness at 1-800-899-2665 or order@msia.org, or visit the MSIA Store online at www.msia.org

Soul Awareness Discourses
A Course in Soul Transcendence

Soul Awareness Discourses are designed to teach Soul Transcendence, which is becoming aware of yourself as a Soul and as one with God—not as a theory, but as a living reality. They are for people who want a consistent, time-proven approach to their spiritual unfoldment.

A set of Soul Awareness Discourses consists of 12 booklets, one to study and contemplate each month of the year. As you read each Discourse, you can activate an awareness of your Soul and deepen your relationship with God.

Spiritual in essence, Discourses are compatible with religious beliefs you might hold. In fact, most people find that Discourses support the experience of whatever path, philosophy, or religion (if any) they choose to follow. Simply put, Discourses are about eternal truths and the wisdom of the spiritual heart.

The first year of Discourses addresses topics ranging from creating success in the world to working hand in hand with Spirit.

A yearly set of Discourses is regularly $100. MSIA is offering the first year of Discourses at an introductory price of $50. Discourses come with a full, no-questions-asked, money-back guarantee. If at any time you decide this course of study is not right for you, simply return it, and you will promptly receive a full refund.

To order Soul Awareness Discourses, contact the Movement of Spiritual Inner Awareness at 1-800-899-2665 or order@msia.org, or visit the MSIA Store online at www.msia.org

For further information on the work of Dr. John-Roger, and to order books, CDs, and DVDs, please contact:

The Movement of Spiritual Inner Awareness
P.O. Box 513935
Los Angeles, CA 90051
323-737-4055

or visit

www.msia.org
www. john-roger.org
www.mandevillepress.org